SHAKE, RATTLE & ROLL

THE FOUNDERS OF ROCK & ROLL

WORDS BY HOLLY GEORGE-WARREN

PICTURES BY LAURA LEVINE

Houghton Mifflin Company   Boston 2001

Words of love to Jack and Robert
— H.G.-W.

For Sarah, Elliot, and Eva
— L.L.

Introduction

BACK IN THE 1950s, THERE WAS A MUSICAL EARTHQUAKE CALLED ROCK & roll that shook everything up. But this exciting music didn't happen overnight—it was actually centuries in the making. Ancient rhythms originating in Africa first came to America on slave ships hundreds of years earlier. Lyrical melodies traveled from Europe to this country with immigrants. Gradually, in the South and Southwest, where black and white people worked together and heard each other's musical traditions, the rhythms and the melodies merged. So by the early twentieth century, rhythmic call-and-response gospel echoed in Alabama churches, the blues rang out in Mississippi cotton fields, country & western shook the rafters of Texas dance halls, banjo- and fiddle-fueled folk songs soared across Appalachian mountaintops, and rhythm & blues tunes set toes a-tappin' in Chicago hot spots.

Future musicians grew up listening to this smorgasbord of sound. In the 1950s, these young black and white artists blended it all together and cooked up rock & roll. The zesty musical stew was a huge hit among teenagers, who especially loved its energetic dance beats and catchy lingo. Rock & roll exploded and became popular across America at sock hops and concerts, on radio and television, in the movies, on jukeboxes, and on record players. In some cities, police, politicians, parents, and preachers banned rock & roll, claiming its crazy rhythms and naughty lyrics could get kids into trouble. Rock & roll survived, though, and became *the* music of a generation.

To this day, rock critics argue over which song was the very first rock & roll number, but most agree that the fourteen men and women in this book created a sound that changed our culture forever. Nearly all of the popular music we listen to today—from rap to country to metal—can be traced back to these founders of rock & roll. As fore-father Chuck Berry put it in a song: "Hail, hail, rock & roll!"

Bill Haley

(1925–1981)

IN 1953, BILL HALEY, BACKED BY HIS GROUP, THE COMETS, TOOK THE brand-new sound of rock & roll to the pop charts for the very first time with "Crazy, Man, Crazy." Bill started his career in the late 1940s as a singing cowboy, leading the country & western (C&W) bands the Down Homers and the Saddlemen. Then he became a fan of rhythm & blues (R&B) and began mixing the two styles together. That's how "Crazy, Man, Crazy" was hatched.

When teenagers went nuts for the song, Bill decided to change his sound for good. His western-style yodeling gave way to bluesy rock & roll singing. He traded his cowboy shirts for bright plaid jackets and wore his hair with a big round curl on his forehead. The next tunes Bill Haley and His Comets recorded became two of the most famous songs in rock & roll history. He learned "Shake, Rattle and Roll" from the R&B artist who originally sang it, Big Joe Turner. Bill himself wrote "Rock Around the Clock," with its sing-along countdown that started, *"One, two, three o'clock, four o'clock ROCK."* The song got a huge boost when it was featured in the movie *Blackboard Jungle* in 1955. It became the first rock & roll song to reach number one on the pop charts. Other hits followed, including "R-O-C-K" and "See You Later, Alligator."

Though Bill Haley was a grownup, he sang about things teens liked and he spoke their language. This talent and his energetic style made him the very first rock & roll star.

Fats Domino

(b. 1928)

FATS DOMINO, ANOTHER EARLY ROCK & ROLL SINGER, PUT THE SOUND OF New Orleans in his music. Beginning with his 1949 theme song, "The Fat Man," he got people out of their seats and onto their feet: *They call me the Fat Man because I weigh 200 pounds.*

Fats was born Antoine Domino, but the chubby tyke got his nickname soon after he learned to play the piano at age ten. His father was a violinist, but it was his brother-in-law, a guitarist, who showed him how to "tickle the ivories." By the time he was fourteen, Fats was playing at New Orleans hot spots. He was following a rich musical tradition: the Crescent City had produced such legendary piano men as Professor Longhair and James Booker, who played a rhythmic style called boogie-woogie that inspired Fats.

After "The Fat Man" became a smash, Fats's hits were unstoppable. His "Blueberry Hill," "I'm Walkin'," "Blue Monday," "Ain't That a Shame," "Whole Lotta Lovin'," and "Walkin' to New Orleans" all helped to popularize rock & roll nationwide. Lots of people wanted to sound like Fats. A young musician in Philadelphia took a stage name inspired by Fats's: he called himself Chubby Checker and in 1960 he became famous with a dance song called "The Twist." The most important group of the sixties, the Beatles, loved Fats's music, too. He later recorded one of their songs, "Lady Madonna," which was his last hit, in 1968.

Through all his success, Fats remained a family man. He gave each of his eight children a name that started with the letter *A*. He still lives in New Orleans, where he continues to rock & roll.

Antoine "FATS" Domino

b. Feb. 26, 1928

New Orleans, LA

LaVern Baker

(1929–1997)

YOU MIGHT SAY LAVERN BAKER WAS BORN WITH MUSIC IN HER BLOOD. Her aunt, Merline Baker, who used the stage name Memphis Minnie, played guitar and sang the blues. As a young girl, LaVern joined the church choir and eventually grew up to become one of rock & roll's earliest female performers.

LaVern began her career in Chicago nightclubs when she was only seventeen. In those days, she called herself Little Miss Sharecropper, inspired by a singer named Little Miss Cornshucks. To look the part, LaVern wore a big straw hat and a raggedy dress covered in patches. In 1949, her family moved to Detroit, where LaVern made her first record, "Sharecropper Boogie."

The fiery way LaVern belted out her R&B songs influenced the brand-new rock & roll sound. Teenagers loved her "Tweedlee Dee" and "Tra La La," which were R&B hits in 1954. LaVern also sang a rowdy song about a boy named "Jim Dandy." At that time, many white radio stations would not play rhythm & blues by black artists, so white singers covered LaVern's songs and made them into much bigger pop hits. LaVern wrote to her congressman about this unfair system, but it would be several years before a change occurred. Eventually, because so many teenagers demanded to hear black artists' records on the radio, these artists finally got airplay and had their own pop hits. This paved the way for other racial barriers to be broken down, and black and white fans were allowed to dance together at concerts for the first time.

LaVern scored some pop hits in the early 1960s, but in 1969 she moved to the Philippines, where she ran a nightclub. Twenty years later, in 1989, she became famous all over again when she returned to the States and starred in the Broadway show *Black and Blue*. Until she retired because of poor health, LaVern remained a sensational entertainer.

Little Richard

(b. 1932)

WITH THE FERVOR OF A PREACHER AND THE GLAMOUR OF A SHOWGIRL, Little Richard was one of rock & roll's earliest stars. He likes to tell people he invented the sound—and many people believe he did.

Born Richard Penniman in Macon, Georgia, he was one of twelve children. He loved to sing as a child, and he performed in public for the first time at age ten when the great gospel-blues singer and guitarist Sister Rosetta Tharpe invited him to join her onstage. Richard especially liked R&B, but his father, who was a preacher, wanted him to listen to and sing only gospel music. So when he was fourteen, Richard left home and joined a series of traveling minstrel shows, including Sugarfoot Sam from Alabam, the King Brothers Circus, the Tidy Jolly Steppers, and the Broadway Follies. Billed as Little Richard, he thrilled audiences with his high-pitched, loud voice and outrageous show-manship. He met a flamboyant performer named Esquerita, who taught him to play piano and inspired him to wear his hair in a huge, frizzy pompadour and grow a pencil-thin mustache.

Little Richard cut his first record when he was eighteen, but his big break came in 1955 when he landed in New Orleans. There he hit upon a magic formula: rapid-fire piano playing behind nearly nonsensical words that he whooped and hollered in a falsetto voice. His New Orleans recording debut resulted in the smash hit "Tutti-Frutti": *"A wop bop a loo bop a wop bam boom, tutti frutti, oh rooti!"* Little Richard screamed. Wow, what a song! Little Richard followed it with more super-charged numbers, "Long Tall Sally," "Lucille," and "Good Golly Miss Molly."

Though he'd finally become a star, Little Richard surprisingly gave up music in 1957 to preach the gospel. He returned to the stage in 1964, though, and has remained one of rock & roll's most spectacular performers.

Chuck Berry

(b. 1926)

*J*UST LET ME HEAR SOME OF THAT ROCK & ROLL MUSIC, ANY OLE WAY *you choose it,*" Chuck Berry sang in one of the many rock & roll theme songs he wrote in the 1950s. He pioneered the sound with his inventive electric guitar, catchy songs, and expressive voice. In addition to "Rock & Roll Music," Chuck also penned the early rock anthems "Johnny B. Goode" and "Roll Over Beethoven."

Chuck learned to play guitar as a teenager, but he didn't become a professional musician right away. First he worked on the assembly line at a car factory, then he styled hair at a beauty shop. He finally started a band in 1952 that included the great piano player Johnnie Johnson. Originally based in St. Louis, Chuck's trio began playing the Midwest, and three years later they signed with Chess, a Chicago record label that specialized in blues and R&B. Chuck's first hit, "Maybellene," came soon after, in 1955.

Teenagers loved watching Chuck perform. A snappy dresser, he scooted across the stage, walking like a duck while playing his guitar. Chuck's hits specialized in witty lyrics that told a story or expressed teens' love for rock & roll: "Sweet Little Sixteen," "School Day," "Brown-Eyed Handsome Man," "Carol," and "Little Queenie."

One of Chuck's biggest fans in the 1950s was an English teenager named Keith Richards, who became a famous guitarist with the Rolling Stones in the 1960s. You can still hear a little bit of Chuck in almost everything Keith plays. Chuck Berry continues to perform his "Rock & Roll Music" and other songs all over the globe.

Elvis Presley

(1935–1977)

THERE'S ONLY ONE KING OF ROCK & ROLL, AND HIS NAME IS ELVIS Presley. Though people played similar music before him, when he came along, he put his unique stamp on the sound and brought it to everyone across America. He made rock & roll popular around the world.

Elvis grew up poor in the small town of Tupelo, Mississippi. He loved music as a child and, at age nine, won second prize at the county fair for his rendition of "Old Shep," a country weeper about a dead dog. Elvis moved to Memphis, Tennessee, with his parents, Vernon and Gladys, when he was a teenager. There he heard different kinds of music: gospel, blues, rhythm & blues, and country & western, all of which would influence his own style. In the beginning, people called his musical blend "rockabilly," a combination of the terms "rock & roll" and "hillbilly."

After graduating from high school, Elvis got a job driving a truck. He saved enough money to buy his mother a special present—he recorded two songs at the Memphis Recording Service, home of Sun Records. The owner, Sam Phillips, who really liked Elvis's distinctive voice, signed him to his label. Elvis began playing with guitarist Scotty Moore, bassist Bill Black, and eventually drummer D. J. Fontana. Elvis's early hits included "That's All Right, Mama," "Good Rockin' Tonight," and "Baby Let's Play House." Dressed in flashy clothes, Elvis drove audiences crazy by swiveling his hips and doing other dance moves when he sang. Girls screamed when he sneered and pouted.

He outgrew tiny Sun Records, moving on to the big national company RCA, where he scored smash after smash: "Heartbreak Hotel," "Blue Suede Shoes," "Don't Be Cruel," "Hound Dog," "Love Me Tender," and "Teddy Bear."

After serving two years in the army, from 1958 to 1960, Elvis stopped performing live and instead starred in musical movies. Finally he returned to the stage in the 1970s. Though he was older and heavier, his fans adored him anyway. After he died in 1977, his legend continued to grow. And he's still the King.

Bo Diddley

(b. 1928)

Can you imagine inventing a guitar riff so important to rock & roll that it's named after you? That's what happened to Bo Diddley. The syncopated Bo Diddley beat sounds like this: *THUMP-a-THUMP-a-THUMP, a-THUMP-THUMP.*

Born Ellas Bates in the Mississippi Delta, Bo was adopted as a baby and his last name was changed to McDaniel. Like many other struggling sharecroppers, he and his family moved to Chicago in search of a better life. There Bo studied violin. Soon he was nicknamed Bo Diddley by his classmates. Down South, people who couldn't afford to buy a real instrument would play music by plucking wires attached to nails hammered into a piece of wood. They called this a diddley bow. That's probably how the kids came up with Bo's name.

Bo learned to build violins and guitars, and when he became a teenager, he switched from playing violin to playing guitar. He started performing on the streets of Chicago and then in the blues clubs. His first hit, "Bo Diddley," helped to make his name famous in 1955. Other hits soon followed: "I'm a Man," "Say Man," and "You Can't Judge a Book by the Cover." These songs were all variations on his Bo Diddley beat. He played a rectangular guitar, and his band included his half-sister, "the Duchess," on guitar and Jerome Green on bass and maracas.

The kind of rhythm & blues Bo Diddley played was a big influence on the developing rock & roll sound. In the 1960s, his songs were covered by the Yardbirds, the Rolling Stones, the Doors, and other rock groups. Thousands of bands have played songs with the Bo Diddley beat.

Bo Diddley is in his seventies now, but he still enjoys touring the country, knocking out that famous *THUMP-a-THUMP-a-THUMP* on his cool guitar.

BO

THE
DUCHESS

DIDDLEY

b. Ellas Bates, 1928

Carl Perkins

(1932–1998)

ONE OF THE GREATEST GUITAR PLAYERS IN ROCK & ROLL HISTORY, CARL Perkins was also an excellent singer and songwriter. His "Blue Suede Shoes" holds up as a rock classic.

Carl grew up in a sharecropping family in rural Tennessee. When he was six, he helped out by picking cotton. In the fields, an old man who played the blues taught Carl how to pick the guitar. In his spare time Carl loved listening to the Grand Ole Opry radio broadcast, especially the bluegrass of Bill Monroe. As a teenager, Carl formed a group with his brothers, bassist Clayton and rhythm guitarist Jay. Carl played electric guitar, sang with a hearty voice, and wrote up-tempo songs that combined his influences of blues, country, and gospel. Soon this new style would be called rockabilly and Carl would be called the Hillbilly Cat.

After tearing up the local roadhouses for a few years, the Perkins brothers traveled to Memphis to seek their fortune at Sun Records. Carl wrote their first single, "Movie Magg," when he was fourteen. Another original song was inspired by something he witnessed at a gig one night: a gussied-up teenage boy warned his dancing partner not to "step on my blue suede shoes." Carl wrote the lyrics to "Blue Suede Shoes" on a paper bag at three in the morning. It became a smash, and Carl and his band were invited to perform the song on a TV show in New York. On the way there, they had a serious car accident, and while the brothers were out of commission, Elvis released his version of the song, which rocketed to number one.

When Carl eventually recovered, his popularity had waned. His songs remained favorites of other musicians, though; "Matchbox," "Honey, Don't," and "Everybody's Trying to Be My Baby" were particular favorites of the Beatles, who recorded several of Carl's songs. Carl went on to tour with Johnny Cash and record country songs before returning to rockabilly, eventually playing with a younger generation of rockers, including two of his sons.

The Everly Brothers

(Don, b. 1937; Phil, b. 1939)

KENTUCKY-BORN BROTHERS DON AND PHIL EVERLY STARTED SINGING together almost as soon as they could talk. Their parents, Ike and Margaret, toured the South playing C&W music, and the boys became part of the act at a young age. By the time they were teenagers, Phil and Don had begun recording together as the Everly Brothers. Their hits blended country and rock & roll and inspired many future vocal groups, including Simon and Garfunkel.

The Everly Brothers first struck out on their own as songwriters in Nashville, where sixteen-year-old Don wrote a hit, "Thou Shalt Not Steal," for country star Kitty Wells. Two years later, Don and Phil recorded "Bye Bye Love," written by a husband-and-wife team. The single shot up to the top ten on the country, R&B, and pop charts, propelling the brothers to stardom.

For five years, they scored hit after hit, including "Wake Up Little Susie," "Bird Dog," and "Cathy's Clown." For their concerts, the handsome duo usually dressed in snazzy matching sport coats and wore their hair the same way, so it was hard to tell them apart. Their voices harmonized perfectly, as only brothers' can. They also squabbled, as brothers often do.

The Everly Brothers continued to perform as a twosome until the 1970s, when they decided to go their separate ways. Linda Ronstadt's recording of their song "When Will I Be Loved" became a huge hit in 1976, and the brothers got back together a few years later. Once in a while they return to the stage to sing their gorgeous duets.

Jerry Lee Lewis

(b. 1935)

ONE OF THE GREATEST SHOWMEN IN ROCK & ROLL, JERRY LEE LEWIS didn't just play the piano and sing, he practically did tricks: jumping up in the air, pounding the keys with his feet, and growling and yodeling his songs. His early records were credited to "Jerry Lee Lewis and His Pumping Piano."

Growing up in Ferriday, Louisiana, Jerry Lee started playing piano when he was eight years old. One day he sat down and played his aunt's piano so well that his mother and father mortgaged their house to buy him one. He practiced constantly and also learned the songs from his parents' records, particularly the yodeling blues of Jimmie Rodgers and Gene Autry. When Jerry Lee was thirteen, he performed in public for the first time at the local Ford dealership. His aunt passed the hat and he earned fifteen dollars. After high school, Jerry Lee gave up music and went to Bible school to become a preacher. But his love of boogie-woogie and the blues had too strong a pull on him, and soon he was back, sneaking into juke joints and learning more tunes.

In 1956 he traveled to Memphis to join the ranks at Sun Records. He and his father raised chickens and sold hundreds of eggs to finance the trip. He recorded the hit "Crazy Arms" and also provided piano accompaniment for other Sun artists' records. The next year he cut his signature number, "Whole Lotta Shakin' Going On," followed by the even wilder "Great Balls of Fire," with Jerry Lee hollering *Goodness, gracious, great balls of fire!* Legend has it that during one show he actually set his piano aflame.

Since those days, he's played all kinds of songs, including a country version of "Chantilly Lace," which was originally done by the Big Bopper, another early rock & roll star. Jerry Lee's version kicks off with *Helloooooooooo, baby, this is the Killer speaking.* Jerry Lee got the nickname "Killer" when he was a boy, because that was the name he called everyone else—and he still does!

Today, when he's not performing, Jerry Lee spends his time on his Mississippi ranch, where he looks after numerous dogs, including five Chihuahuas that he calls "the family jewels."

TOO MUCH LOVING DRIVES A MAN INSANE
YOU BROKE MY WILL OH WHAT A THRILL
GOODNESS GRACIOUS GREAT BALLS OF FIRE
YOU SHAKE MY NERVES AND YOU RATTLE MY BRAIN
JERRY LEE LEWIS
THE "KILLER"
L. LEVINE

Buddy Holly

(1936–1959)

*P*EGGY SUE, PEGGY SUE, PRET-TY, PRET-TY, PRET-TY, PRET-TY PEG-GY SUE," sang Buddy Holly with his band, the Crickets, in 1957. Buddy, who was born Charles Hardin Holley in Lubbock, Texas, set the style for 1960s rock bands by writing most of the songs played by his group, which consisted of electric guitar, bass, and drums. In the 1950s, pop, country, and R&B singers usually were backed by session musicians hired by the record label and sang tunes written by professional songwriters. Buddy and the Crickets changed things by doing almost everything themselves, as they did on "Peggy Sue."

As a teenager, Buddy played C&W but discovered rock & roll after he shared a bill with Elvis. Buddy had a special voice that could hiccup and chirp, and it sounded good singing all types of music: fast, slow, country & western, rhythm & blues, and especially rock & roll. Some say that his group got their name from a cricket that chimed in when the boys practiced in Buddy's garage.

After the Crickets became successful in 1957 with their first hit, "That'll Be the Day," Buddy moved to New York. More hits followed, including "Oh Boy," "Maybe Baby," and "Rave On." Sadly, Buddy was killed only seventeen months after he became a star. His plane crashed during a blizzard following a concert at the Surf Ballroom in Clear Lake, Iowa. But he and his music will never be forgotten. Since his death, count-less artists have cited his songs as a big influence on their own music. The Beatles named themselves after a bug—a beetle—in honor of Buddy's Crickets. Another British group called their band the Hollies, for Buddy.

Most important, Buddy's songs have been kept alive by other musicians who play them. One of Buddy's song titles, later recorded by such bands as the Rolling Stones and the Grateful Dead, sums up his musical legacy—"Not Fade Away."

Wanda Jackson

(b. 1937)

BﾠACK WHEN ROCK & ROLL BELONGED TO THE BOYS, A FRISKY YOUNG female singer burst onto the scene. Wanda Jackson's unique voice and dynamic stage presence showed the world that gals could rock! And none other than Elvis Presley gave Wanda his seal of approval.

Wanda Jackson first appeared onstage in her home state of Oklahoma when she was just nine years old. Her father and mother loved country music, especially western swing and honky-tonk, styles that developed in Texas in the 1940s. They took young Wanda with them to see groups perform in Oklahoma and California, where the family moved when Wanda was ten. Her father taught her to play guitar and piano, and her robust singing impressed grownups, teenagers, and kids her age. When she was thirteen, Wanda got her own radio show.

Originally, Wanda sang country songs on bills with such C&W stars as Hank Thompson. One night, in 1955, she gigged with Elvis Presley. He loved Wanda's performance and told her that she had the perfect voice for singing rockabilly. At his urging, she changed her act, learned some new material, and even began writing her own songs. One of her most festive numbers, "Let's Have a Party," became a hit in 1960, two years after Wanda first recorded it and after Elvis sang it in a movie.

Elvis's colorful wardrobe impressed Wanda, so she ditched her cowgirl outfits and began wearing skintight dresses, sewed by her mother, that were accented with fringe and sparkly rhinestones that shimmied and shook. As Wanda belted out such raucous tunes as "Hot Dog," "Fujiyama Mama," and the self-penned "Mean Mean Man," she danced around the stage—unlike the usually demure girl singers of the day.

Today, Wanda Jackson is known as the Queen of Rockabilly for breaking down the barriers that had prevented women from performing with gusto like the guys. She still goes on the road, singing her catchy rockabilly songs to audiences around the world. And she still wears fringe.

Ritchie Valens

(1941–1959)

RITCHIE VALENS BROUGHT ELEMENTS OF MEXICAN MUSIC TO ROCK & roll. He was just sixteen when he became a professional musician. Only one year later, he met a tragic death.

Ritchie, born Richard Stephen Valenzuela, came from a very poor Mexican-American family in California's San Fernando Valley. His father played Latin-style guitar, so young Ritchie started strumming along on a ukulele or toy guitar. Soon he could play for real, and he also learned trumpet, harmonica, and drums. He often babysat for his brothers and sisters and would play music to entertain them. When he was in high school, he became the lead singer and guitarist for a band called the Silhouettes. The group covered so many Little Richard songs that Ritchie got the nickname Little Richard of the Valley. In 1958, a friend passed along a tape of a Silhouettes' show to the owner of a recording studio, who really liked Ritchie's melodic voice, rock & roll guitar–playing, and his original song "Come On, Let's Go," inspired by an expression his family often used. They cut the song, and it became Ritchie's first hit.

The next year, Ritchie composed a beautiful love song about his girlfriend, Donna.

For the flip side of "Donna," he played a tune inspired by traditional Mexican wedding music. He sang "La Bamba" in Spanish after his aunt taught him the words. "La Bamba" is probably the most famous Spanish song in American pop history. With the money he earned from the record's success, Ritchie bought his mother a house.

To promote his music, Ritchie often appeared on TV shows and rock & roll package tours. On February 3, 1959, he performed at the Winter Dance Party in Clear Lake, Iowa, with Buddy Holly and the Big Bopper. That night he played drums with Holly, whose regular drummer was sick. After the show, Ritchie, Buddy, and the Bopper boarded a tiny plane bound for Minnesota. When the airplane crashed that night, the world lost three of its best rock & rollers. Thanks to a 1972 folk-rock song called "American Pie," we still remember that sad occasion as *the day the music died.*

James Brown

(b. 1933)

JAMES BROWN HAS MANY NICKNAMES, ONE OF WHICH IS "THE HARDEST Working Man in Show Business." For fifty years, he's been knocking audiences dead with his amazing voice and spectacular stage moves.

James Brown had it rough as a little kid. His mother left the family when he was a baby, so he lived in a shack in the woods with his father. It was very lonely, but at age five, James learned to play the harmonica to entertain himself. When he was six, he moved to Augusta, Georgia, to his great-aunt's house. Because they were poor, little James had to pick cotton and peanuts, cut sugarcane, and shine shoes to earn money. He also formed his first band, called the Cremona Trio. Eventually, he fell in with a bad crowd and became a burglar. When he was sixteen, he was arrested and sent to a special jail for teenagers. There he met a gospel musician named Bobby Byrd, who performed for the inmates. After three years, young James got out and moved in with Bobby's family. At first, James tried to become a boxer, then a baseball player. He found his true calling when he and Bobby sang gospel together.

One night they performed on a bill with some new rock & roll acts, including Fats Domino. James and Bobby loved the style so much they started their own group called the Flames. In 1956, the Flames scored their first hit, "Please, Please, Please." Soon everyone knew James Brown and his Famous Flames for their gospel-meets-rhythm & blues sound, and for James's magnificent dancing onstage. People started calling him Mr. Dynamite. Supposedly, he lost seven pounds during every show because of his high-energy performance.

The exciting rhythms of James Brown's music gave birth to the sound of soul, an R&B style that became very hot in the 1960s. By the mid-1960s, James had earned yet another nickname, "Soul Brother Number One." His influence didn't stop there. He also pioneered the 1970s black music style called funk, and beginning in the 1980s James would influence rap, the most popular new sound since the birth of rock & roll.

Text copyright © 2001 by Holly George-Warren
Illustrations copyright © 2001 by Laura Levine

All rights reserved. For information about permission
to reproduce selections from this book, write to
Permissions, Houghton Mifflin Company,
215 Park Avenue South, New York, New York 10003.

www.houghtonmifflinbooks.com

Many thanks to Bob George and the ARChive of Contemporary Music

The text of this book is set in 14-point Berthold Bodoni Antiqua.
The paintings are acrylic/mixed media on masonite.

Library of Congress Cataloging-in-Publication Data

George-Warren, Holly.
Shake, rattle & roll : the founders of rock & roll /
written by Holly George-Warren ; illustrated by Laura Levine.
p.   cm.
ISBN 0-618-05540-1
1. Rock musicians – Biography – Juvenile literature.
[1. Rock musicians.] I. Levine, Laura, 1958–   ill.
ML3929 .G46   2001
781.66'092'2 – dc21
[B]
00-033480

Manufactured in the United States of America
BVG 10 9 8 7 6 5 4 3 2 1